Frogs

مینڈک

Macdonald

A MACDONALD BOOK

© Macdonald & Co (Publishers) Ltd 1987

This dual language edition first published
in Great Britain in 1987

English edition first published in 1971
New English edition published in 1986

Dual language text editor: Jennie Ingham
Translated into Urdu by Qamar Zamani
Urdu adviser: Farmanullah Khan Kashif
Urdu translation © Jennie Ingham Associates Ltd 1987
Dual text layout design by Jennie Ingham Associates Ltd
64-68 Camden High Street, London NW1 0LT, England

British Library Cataloguing in Publication Data
Frogs. – (Starters Urdu)
    1. Urdu language – Readers
    491'.43986421   PK1975

    ISBN 0-356-13651-5

Printed in Great Britain by
Purnell Book Production Ltd
Member of the BPCC Group

Published by Macdonald & Co (Publishers) Ltd,
Greater London House
Hampstead Road
London NW1 7QX

Members of BPCC plc

Illustrator: Isobel Beard

میڈک پانی کے قریب رہتے ہیں ۔

وہ پانی میں تیرتے ہیں ۔

وہ بہت اچھے تیراک ہوتے ہیں ۔

Frogs live near water.
They swim in the water.
They can swim well.

مینڈک زمین پر بھی رہ سکتے ہیں ۔

وہ ایسی جگہ رہتے ہیں جہاں نمی ہو ۔

Frogs can stay on land too.
They stay where it is damp.

مینڈک کودنے میں ماہر ہیں ۔

ان کے پچھلے پیر لمبے ہوتے ہیں ۔

ان کی لمبی ٹانگیں انہیں کودنے میں مدد دیتی ہیں ۔

Frogs jump well.
They have long back legs.
Their long legs help them to jump.

The female frog is bigger
than the male frog.
The male frog croaks.

In spring the mother frog
lays some eggs in the pond.
The eggs are in jelly.
The jelly keeps the eggs safe.

انڈوں میں سے مینڈک کے بچے یعنی ٹیڈپول نکلتے ہیں ۔

ٹیڈپول کا سَر بڑا اور دُم لمبی

ہوتی ہے ۔

شروع شروع میں یہ پودے کھاتا ہے ۔

The eggs hatch into tadpoles.
The tadpole has a big head
and a long tail.
At first it eats plants.

The tadpole grows two back legs.
Then it grows two front legs.

جیسے جیسے وہ بڑھتا ہے اس کی شکل بدلتی جاتی ہے ۔

اس کی دُم غائب ہو جاتی ہے ۔

اب ٹیڈپول ایک

مینڈک کی شکل میں تبدیل ہوچکا ہے ۔

As it grows it changes shape.
It loses its tail.
Now the tadpole
has turned into a little frog.

یہ چھوٹا سا مینڈک بڑھتا چلا جاتا ہے ۔

اس کی کھال پھٹنے لگتی ہے ۔

اس پُرانی کھال کے نیچے ایک نئی کھال ہے ۔

مینڈک اپنی پُرانی کھال اتار دیتا ہے اور اُسے کھا جاتا ہے ۔

The little frog gets bigger and bigger.
Its skin splits.
There is a new skin under the old one.
The frog pulls off the old skin and eats it.

سردیوں میں مینڈک سو جاتا ہے ۔

وہ تالاب کی کیچڑ میں سوتا ہے ۔

وہ کھانا نہیں کھاتا ۔

صرف اپنی کھال کے ذریعہ سانس لیتا رہتا ہے ۔

In winter the frog sleeps.
It sleeps in the mud in the pond.
It does not eat.
It breathes through its skin.

In spring it is warm again.
The frog wakes up.
The frog looks for food.

11

مینڈک چھوٹے چھوٹے پانی کے جانور کھاتا ہے ۔

وہ کیڑے بھی کھاتا ہے ۔

تتلی
butterfly

ڈیڈی لونگ لیگنز
daddy longlegs

بیبر بہوٹی
ladybird

لال بیگ
beetle

کیڑا
worm

گھونگا
snail

سلگ
slug

The frog eats small water animals.
It also eats insects.

The frog has a long sticky tongue.
The frog catches insects with its tongue.

سب سے چھوٹا مینڈک
smallest frog

دیو پیکر مینڈک
giant frog

There are more than two thousand
kinds of frog.
The giant frog is forty centimetres long.
The smallest frog is one centimetre long.

Some frogs live in trees.
Tree frogs have suckers on their toes.
The suckers help them climb trees.

Some tree frogs can change colour.
When it sits on a leaf it is green.
When it sits on a branch it is brown.
It changes colour to keep it safe.

Some frogs can jump a very long way.
They are called flying frogs.
They do not really fly.
They just jump.

This frog is called an edible frog.
It is croaking.

18

This frog has two bumps over its eyes.
They look like horns.
It is called the horned frog.

Some frogs have poison on their skin.
The poison keeps other animals away.

بعض جانور اپنے کھانے کے لئے مینڈک پکڑتے ہیں ۔

بعض چڑیاں بھی مینڈک کھاتی ہیں ۔

شکرہ
hawk

بگلا
heron

سٹوٹ
stoat

سانپ
snake

خارپشت
hedgehog

بطخ
duck

لومڑی
fox

Some animals catch frogs to eat.
Some birds eat frogs too.

موسم بہار میں کچھ مینڈک کے انڈوں کی تلاش کرو ۔

ان کو تالاب کے پانی میں رکھو ۔

دیکھو کہ انڈوں میں سے ٹیڈپول کس طرح نکلتے ہیں ۔

ٹیڈپول مینڈک میں تبدیل ہو جائیں گے ۔

See for yourself
In spring look for some frogs' eggs.
Keep them in some pond water.
Watch the eggs hatch into tadpoles.
The tadpoles will turn into frogs.

ٹارٹرکے مینڈک کے متعلق الفاظ

Starter's **Frogs** words

پچھلی ٹانگیں

back legs
(page 3)

تتلی

butterfly
(page 12)

انڈے

eggs
(page 5)

کیڑا

worm
(page 12)

تالاب

pond
(page 5)

لال بیگ

beetle
(page 12)

ٹیڈ پول

tadpole
(page 6)

گھونگا

snail
(page 12)

پودا

plant
(page 6)

زبان

tongue
(page 13)

درختوں کا مینڈک

tree frog
(page 15)

چپکنے والی گدیاں

suckers
(page 15)

پنجے

toes
(page 15)

پتّہ

leaf
(page 16)

شاخ

branch
(page 16)

اُڑنے والا مینڈک

flying frog
(page 17)

کھائے جانے والا مینڈک

edible frog
(page 18)

سینگ والا مینڈک

horned frog
(page 19)

خارپشت

hedgehog
(page 21)

بگلا

heron
(page 21)